Original title:
A Journey Through Life's Absurdities

Copyright © 2025 Creative Arts Management OÜ
All rights reserved.

Author: Arabella Whitmore
ISBN HARDBACK: 978-1-80566-107-8
ISBN PAPERBACK: 978-1-80566-402-4

Letters from the Land of Unreason

In a land where socks do dance at night,
And toasters dream of taking flight,
The trees wear hats, the rocks all chat,
While cats recite the tales of that.

One day a snail declares he'll race,
And leaves the turtles in their place,
With every step, he shakes his head,
"I've got nowhere to be!" he said.

The moon forgot to rise on time,
It's busy writing folksy rhyme,
With stars that giggle, cheeky and bright,
As comets play hopscotch in the night.

The clouds wear shoes made of candy cane,
And puddles giggle when it rains,
A rubber chicken leads the parade,
Where nothing truly gets remade.

Illusions on the Horizon

On the road I found a shoe,
Its mate was lost, what's it to do?
I asked a squirrel, 'Have you seen?'
He chattered back, 'Just living the dream.'

A signpost points to nowhere right,
With directions drawn in crayon, bright.
I took a left, then found a right,
Now I'm dancing with clouds tonight.

Medleys of the Misfit

A cat with glasses reads the news,
While dogs debate their favorite shoes.
A toad plays chess with a bumblebee,
They argue loudly, who's best, you see?

The jester juggles freshly baked pies,
While the wise old owl just rolls his eyes.
The world is bizarre, a grand old jest,
Where the oddest creatures feel quite blessed.

Fleeting Moments of Merriment

A snail once raced a rabbit bold,
The tales of glory, forever told.
They'd laugh and cheer at sunset's glow,
While the worms played tunes on ukulele, yo!

A rainbow erupted, a cactus sang,
The flowers danced, their petals sprang.
Together they laughed through silly strife,
What a riot, this thing called life!

Between Logic and Lunacy

A penguin wears a polka-dot tie,
While pondering why the fish all fly.
He flips through pages of nonsense prose,
And wonders why the chicken chose.

The clocks spin backward, the dogs recite,
Poems of nonsense, what a sight!
In a world askew, where laughter's key,
I'll toast to absurdity, join me, shall we?

Whispers of the Wayward

In a land where socks go missing,
And fruit flies hold debates,
Kittens rule the afternoon,
While dogs pen their own fates.

Balloons float with secret dreams,
While sandwiches feel shy,
Chickens work in office jobs,
As cows stare at the sky.

The sun wears a silly hat,
In a world upside down,
Llamas knit their scarves in peace,
While goats wear tiny crowns.

Through puddles of chocolate rain,
And whispers full of glee,
We laugh through all the madness,
In this crazy jubilee.

Fractured Fairy Tales

In a forest made of jellybeans,
Where mermaids sing off-key,
A prince got stuck in bubblegum,
And danced with a bumblebee.

Cinderella lost her glass shoe,
To a raccoon on the run,
While Rapunzel's hair was tangled,
In a tangle of spun fun.

The wolf now brews espresso,
With Grandma in a café,
While three pigs build their houses,
Out of straws and hip hoorays.

The moon wears sparkly slippers,
And twirls around the stars,
As dwarfs juggle with cupcakes,
And chuckle in their cars.

Fluctuations of the Fabled

A dragon stole a pair of shoes,
To dance across the skies,
While witches brew their coffee,
And giggle at their pies.

The princess ate a pickle,
To grant her wiggle power,
And frogs are hatching plans today,
To eat a magic flower.

Goblins traded shiny rocks,
For beans that grow so tall,
But each time they climbed higher,
They slipped on pudding's sprawl.

The castle's full of rubber ducks,
That float in royal pools,
While knights wear polka-dot armor,
And break all of the rules.

The Dance of the Ridiculous

With jester hats and goofy shoes,
We twirl upon the ground,
The trees clap hands with glee,
As laughter echoes 'round.

Cats hold tea parties at noon,
As they sip from thimbles bright,
While raccoons juggle fireflies,
Beneath the twinkling night.

The clouds wear striped pajamas,
As rain falls like confetti,
And every hill's a slide today,
Where silliness is petty.

In this carnival of whimsies,
Join the fun, don't be shy,
For in the dance of nonsense,
We're all meant to fly.

The Quirky Dance of Existence

In a world where socks mismatch,
Dancing shoes get tangled, oh what a catch!
Laughter spills like lemonade,
As we twirl through truths that never fade.

Umbrella fights on sunny days,
Chasing clouds that wear a gaze.
We glide on banana peels with glee,
What a sight, just wait and see!

Whispers of Wobbling Reality

The cat wears glasses, oh what a scene,
Chasing invisible mice, if you know what I mean.
Teapots sing in the middle of night,
While stars juggle dreams with delight.

Get lost in a maze made of cheese,
Finding crumbs that tease and please.
Our boots tap dance on a melting floor,
Who knew life had so much in store?

Serendipity in the Silly

A circus of thoughts, all dressed in a hat,
Balloons float by, imagine that!
Giggles form rainbows in the sky,
As rubber ducks on bicycles zoom by.

The fridge talks back, what a surprise,
While pickles debate with the fries.
Hilarious truths take flight and swirl,
In a nonsense dance, a merry whirl.

Maps Drawn in Crayon

With crayon maps and colors bold,
Adventure awaits in stories told.
We'll navigate by the stars' silly winks,
And solve the puzzles that life throws, I think!

On sidewalks drawn, we skip and hop,
Chasing dreams straight to the top.
Where every mishap becomes a laugh,
Wandering paths with a goofy path!

The Circuitous Sojourn

With every turn, we lose the map,
Yet laugh and dance, in this mishap.
A sock on the head, a shoe on the hand,
We twirl through the grass, with no clear plan.

Lost in a shop filled with rubber ducks,
I barter my hat for strange little lucks.
The path we took was never the right,
But joy found its way, in the baffling night.

Laughing Through the Labyrinth

In a maze of mirrors, who do I see?
Do they really reflect, or just mock me?
I trip on the thoughts that escape my head,
Chasing a pigeon, wishing I fled.

With each wrong turn, a giggle erupts,
As I try to avoid what the world corrupts.
I stumble and tumble, a sight to behold,
Life's silly antics, more precious than gold.

Odyssey of Odd

Pancakes for shoes, and jelly for hats,
My friends are all talking to very small rats.
We fly on the backs of well-dressed bears,
With buttered popcorn and giggly stares.

Downward we tumble, but upwards we soar,
In this circus of chaos, we crave even more.
Life wears a mask, painted with cheer,
Join this odd play; pull up a chair!

Encounters with the Unorthodox

A talking cactus gave me some zest,
Its tales of adventure are simply the best.
I sipped on a smoothie made from the sky,
With rainbows for straws—oh my, oh my!

On top of a cloud, we played tag with the sun,
Life's bizarre moments have only begun.
In this grand theater, laughter's the thread,
Embrace all the wackiness, let joy be widespread.

Where the Bizarre Blooms

In a land where socks talk back,
And milkshakes dance with glee,
The trees wear hats of polka dots,
While ants sip tea by the sea.

A cat with shoes throws a fit,
As rainbows fall like sprinkles,
A turtle on a skateboard zooms,
While laughing at the wrinkles.

The sun decides to take a nap,
As jellybeans float on by,
A cloud gets lost in a pizza slice,
And seagulls wear bow ties.

So join the fun, don't hesitate,
Embrace the quirks, the charms,
For in this world of weird delight,
We find the sweet, warm arms.

Daffodils in the Mist of Madness

Daffodils play cards with grass,
While crickets hum a tune,
A cupcake rides a bicycle,
Underneath a bright blue moon.

Pineapples debate on the street,
About who's the best fruit king,
While jellyfish juggle jellybeans,
And frogs learn how to sing.

The clocks melt on the garden wall,
Where rabbits cook with flair,
Marshmallow clouds drift lazily,
In a flavor of fresh air.

So let's dance with wild mushrooms,
And twirl with silly snails,
In a circus made of wonder,
Where reason always fails.

The Symptom of Serendipity

In a world where moons wear shoes,
And teabags float in space,
A penguin twirls in polka dots,
With a rather silly grace.

Pancakes rain from fluffy skies,
As squirrels sell cotton candy,
A goat rides on a rollercoaster,
While shouting, "Isn't that dandy?"

The sun plays peek-a-boo with clouds,
While butterflies paint the air,
A sandwich dreams of being free,
But finds it just too rare.

So throw your doubts into the wind,
And let the laughter spread,
For in this wacky carnival,
Life laughs at what we dread.

Paradoxes at Dusk

At dusk where shadows tell tales,
And fish wear little hats,
The moon scribbles on the ground,
While raccoons play baseball bats.

A dog recites a poem loud,
As trees grow arms to dance,
While unicorns in polka dots,
Take turns with fate and chance.

The whispers of a laughing breeze,
Carry secrets just for fun,
As bicycles race against the wind,
And rainbows start to run.

So leap into the strange and wild,
And spin a tale or two,
For in this realm of paradox,
Absurdity shines through.

The Sideshow of Self-Discovery

Step right up, can't you see,
Each clown reflects some part of me.
A jester's hat, a fortune told,
In every laugh, a truth unfolds.

Balancing acts and pratfalls keen,
The brightest colors seldom seen.
With pie in face and slapstick sound,
In chaos, wisdom can be found.

Horns honk loud, the crowd will cheer,
Illusions vanish, yet we draw near.
In this circus, life unfolds,
Where laughter's worth more than gold.

Step right up, let's take a chance,
Embrace the weird in every dance.
In painted smiles, we'll find our grace,
A sideshow mirror, our true face.

The Playful Paradox

In every riddle, a twist appears,
The wise crack jokes, the foolish sneers.
Tickle your mind, unravel the seams,
What seems absurd can fuel our dreams.

A cat in a hat, a fish in a shoe,
Wonders abound, the bizarre is true.
With logic upside down and inside out,
We stroll through life without a doubt.

Laughter wraps around each fable,
Wit is the key to this absurd label.
The quietest minds hold the loudest laughs,
In this playful world, we make our paths.

So wear your quirks like a badge of fun,
Dance with the chaos, let's all run.
In paradox, we find our way,
Through the whimsical shades of every day.

The Unsung Symphony of Silly

A symphony plays on a rubber duck,
Each note a giggle, pure stroke of luck.
With tickled ivories and cymbals bright,
The sound of joy, a silly delight.

Banana peels and dancing shoes,
Life's a song, so don't refuse.
Off-key notes, yet harmony flows,
In laughter's echo, our spirit grows.

Trombones slide in a wobbly tune,
While squirrels waltz beneath the moon.
Where seriousness fades into a blur,
In this orchestra, let's all concur.

So raise a glass to absurd design,
Grab a kazoo, it's party time.
In the symphony of the wacky and wild,
We find our rhythm, just like a child.

The Erratic Escapade

Off we go, with mismatched shoes,
A map that's torn, a guide with clues.
Winding paths, we skip and trip,
In every stumble, gems we grip.

A goat on a skateboard, zooming fast,
Madcap moments that never last.
With laughter echoing down the lane,
Absurdity's joy, a sweet refrain.

Through fields of daisies, we chase the breeze,
Jumping over fences, doing as we please.
With every twist, life's plot unfolds,
A tale of wonders, forever told.

So grab a friend, let's run amok,
In this escapade, we'll beat the clock.
For in the chaos, we find our spark,
In this wild dance, we leave our mark.

A Tapestry of the Unexpected

In socks of mismatched hues, we dance,
Chasing shadows in a silly prance.
A banana phone rings in mid-air,
Conversations with squirrels, if you dare.

Wearing hats made of spaghetti, we roam,
Searching for meaning in a garden gnome.
Each signpost points to nowhere at all,
Yet still, we stumble, we trip, we fall.

A cat in a top hat leads the way,
While penguins recite poetry at play.
With laughter echoing down the street,
Absurdity makes our lives so sweet.

So let's toast to the quirks we find,
In this crazy tapestry, so entwined.
Every thread a different tale to tell,
Life's oddities weave a magical spell.

The Whimsical Wanderer

A whimsical wanderer skips with glee,
With shoes made of marshmallows, what a sight to see!
They chat with the clouds, share jokes with the sun,
As time frolics by, oh what fun!

Sliding down rainbows, landing in pies,
While fish in bow ties perform a surprise.
Each twist of fate is a cartoonish chase,
Time flies on the back of a colorful space.

With a trumpet that plays the sound of cheese,
They dance with the daisies, float on the breeze.
Laughter paints the sky in crazy colors,
While rabbits in sunglasses cheer for their brothers.

So join this journey, so silly and bright,
For life's little quirks fill the day with delight.
In the land of nonsense, we all belong,
With smiles as our compass, let's sing our song.

Beyond the Boundaries of Reason

Beyond reason's reach, where the moon wears a hat,
A fish plays chess with a curious cat.
Unicorns argue about peanut butter,
While owls in tuxedos sip cocoa and mutter.

The trees tell tales of their wild, windy dreams,
As snails in top hats plot against beams.
Time ticks backward, like a lost little tune,
While chickens in aviators salute the moon.

A clock strikes thirteen, we all take a bow,
As jellybeans march through the town right now.
Each misstep a treasure, each giggle a goal,
In the circus of life, let's play our role.

So let's wander deeper where logic is lost,
Among thrilling absurdities, count not the cost.
With whimsy our guide, take a chance, let's embrace,
The laughter and joy in this wild, funny space.

The Mirth Merchant's Voyage

A mirth merchant sails on a boat full of cheer,
Through giggles and snickers, with friends drawing near.
They barter with laughter, trade smiles for dreams,
While jellyfish dance in the sun's golden beams.

With a map made of candy, they travel afar,
Collecting the oddities, near and far star.
Each port brings a tale, a quirky old sight,
Like dogs that wear hats, oh what a delight!

Potatoes in tuxedos perform on the shore,
As mermaids recite absurd poems galore.
Giggling pirates join in on the fun,
Their treasure: a belly laugh and a bun.

So let's set sail on this whimsical spree,
With the mirth merchant's heart, let's dance by the sea.
Let absurdities guide us, forever we'll roam,
In laughter's embrace, we'll always feel home.

Epiphanies in Absurdity

In a world where cats wear hats,
And squirrels dance in the street,
We stumble on thoughts, oh so flat,
While juggling our breakfast treat.

With socks that never find their pair,
And pants that seem to sprout,
We laugh at life without a care,
As ducks quack rhythmic doubt.

The fish debate in the fishbowl's light,
While table talk gets absurd,
Around the clock, day turns to night,
Time whispers, 'You've not heard.'

So let's toast to the quirks we meet,
With coffee poured into a shoe,
Each moment, a wobbly, quirky feat,
In this madcap hullabaloo.

The Tangents of Time

Woke up today, but wait, wrong day,
The cat's wearing goggles of blue,
A calendar spins, in funny array,
Time's jester tickles us too.

We hop on the bus to who-knows-where,
While chickens chase their own tails,
Life's slide shows a comic affair,
With jokes told by shady snails.

And clocks melt down with a dramatic flair,
As seconds zoom by on a scooter,
Laughter erupts – a madcap air,
Time's narrative grows ever cuter.

So grab your hat and do not mind,
The twists and turns of this ride,
In the chaos, pure joy we find,
As the world spins round with pride.

Chronicles of the Curious

They say a hedgehog sings at night,
While turtles tango with glee,
Pursuing questions, oh what a sight,
Curiosity bursts forth like tea!

With books that fly off the shelves in haste,
And lightbulbs that flicker, unsure,
We giggle, perplexed by life's wild taste,
In this absurd, heady tour.

A platypus reads with glasses askew,
While bees wear a crown made of cream,
Absurd little quirks, old yet new,
As imagination sips on a dream.

So let's twirl through this whimsical spring,
Where questions bloom in a swirl,
In the chronicles of curious things,
Life's humor gives us a whirl.

Dances with Dissonance

Oh, what a party in the trees,
Where owls and raccoons tap a beat,
In a clumsy jig that brings us to knees,
As absurdy tunes make life sweet.

Penguins slide in tuxedoed grace,
While dolphins strum on a lute,
Each note a laugh, a funny chase,
Inviting us in to join the loot.

As a giraffe leads with wobbly flair,
And bunnies hop in a grand ballet,
We twirl and spin, without a care,
In the wild groove of the day.

So dance with dissonance anew,
Embrace the odd with a grin,
For life's absurd, but isn't it true,
In laughter, we truly win.

Chasing Shadows of the Unusual

In a land where penguins sell ice cream,
I lost my hat while chasing a dream.
The clouds wore pants, the sun had a tie,
And I asked a squirrel, 'How high can you fly?'

With a map drawn by a wandering cat,
I found a door where a fish sat flat.
It gave me directions with a wink and a grin,
To the party of socks that never begin.

Follies Beneath the Stars

Underneath the disco moon, we dance,
With marshmallow feet, we twirl and prance.
A cactus played guitar, oh what a sight,
While rabbits in tuxedos joined in the night.

The owls wore glasses, read poetry aloud,
As we sipped from cups that waved and bowed.
Laughter like bubbles, where chaos is sweet,
In this whimsical world, we never retreat.

The Absurdity Alphabet

A is for acorns that wear little shoes,
B is for balloons that giggle and snooze.
C is a cat riding a bicycle fast,
D is for donuts that run from the past.

E is an ear, listening to cheese,
F is the fountain that burbles with ease.
G is for gardens where gnomes work at night,
Z is for zebras who dream of flight.

Curious Curves of Fate

Life's a slippery slide, painted in stripes,
With fruit that sings softly and offers ripe gripes.
Umbrellas on roller coasters, what a delight,
As shadows of llamas dance into the night.

I met a wise walrus, told me to sit,
He played our future, a jumbled up skit.
With giggles and wiggles that defy every rule,
We rode the odd waves—absurdity's school.

The Kaleidoscope of Life

Colors blur and twist in time,
Each moment a new silly rhyme.
Socks on hands and hats askew,
We waltz through mayhem, just me and you.

Spinning tops and fallen pies,
Funny faces, goofy cries.
A kangaroo with shoes that squeak,
In our parade, joy is unique.

With every giggle and silly dance,
Life's absurdities grant us a chance.
To find delight in what seems strange,
Embracing chaos, we'll never change.

Through the lens of laughter's grace,
Every blunder, a smiling face.
Come join the ride with hearts so light,
In this kaleidoscope, life feels just right!

Revelations in the Ridiculous

Whispers from a flying fish,
Prompt us to take a silly swish.
Finding nuggets of pure delight,
In foolish antics, oh what a sight!

Banana peels on sunny days,
Send us skidding in a million ways.
We stumble, trip, and giggle loud,
In this circus, let's be proud!

Rolling down a hill of fun,
Chasing shadows, we both run.
Life's little quirks, a laughing choir,
Humor ignites our inner fire.

When penguins dance and tigers twirl,
We're caught up in this whirly swirl.
Silly moments, our hearts will keep,
In this wacky world, we'll always leap!

The Labyrinth of Laughter

In a maze made of rubber ducks,
We dodge the bristles of bad luck.
With each corner turned anew,
Laughter echoes, bouncing through.

Juggling cakes and chasing tails,
Riding on the back of snails.
Our map is scribbled, oh what fun!
Every twist feels like a pun.

Through the hedges filled with cheer,
We find the funny lurking near.
Each misstep spins a tale so grand,
In this labyrinth, hand in hand.

With hiccups loud and noses red,
We'll laugh through all that's left unsaid.
Embracing goofiness, side by side,
In this maze of joy, we'll always glide!

Mirthful Mishaps

Tripping over clever cats,
Landing softly on fuzzy mats.
In the chaos, laughs erupt,
Every blunder, joy corrupt.

Waving at birds that stole our fries,
With sparkly dreams and goofy eyes.
Life's a comedy, so let's rehearse,
Through mishaps, we'll break the curse.

Falling into puddles of surprise,
Dancing with umbrellas in the skies.
Each splatter a brand new chance,
In these goofy moments, let's prance.

Giggles swirling all around,
In funny tales, friendships are found.
Through every mishap, joy we weave,
In this mirthful mess, we believe!

Twilight's Topsy-Turvy Tales

In a world where chickens fly,
And fish can dance beneath the sky,
The clock strikes twelve, yet it's noon,
While cats recite a silly tune.

Pies float by on miniature balloons,
While cats debate the merits of spoons.
A frog wears a crown, calls himself king,
And croaks the anthem our hearts will sing.

The trees wear hats, all bright and loud,
As squirrels form a tiny crowd.
With acorns small, they hold a feast,
Embracing lunacy, at least!

So laugh, my friend, at life so bright,
Where nothing seems to feel quite right.
Embrace the weird, let spirits soar,
In twilight's tales, there's always more.

The Curious Side of Chaos

Underneath a sky of purple sheep,
A sleepy worm tries not to leap.
The sun shines green, the clouds are red,
While carrots chatter in my head.

A fish in sneakers jogs around,
While rabbits listen to music's sound.
The moon paints stripes on wandering trees,
As butterflies join in a breeze.

The ants parade in fancy hats,
Debating if they should eat or chat.
Jellybeans rain down from above,
And all things quirky, we shall love.

So if you trip on gummy bears,
And dance with ducks in silly pairs,
Just smile brightly, let laughter flow,
In chaos' arms, let whimsy grow.

Echoes from the Eccentric

A penguin wearing shades goes by,
On roller skates, oh my oh my!
He waves hello to the flying cows,
As hedgehogs dance in silly bows.

The sun's a lemon, tart and bright,
Its rays in spirals, what a sight!
It tickles flowers to make them laugh,
In rivers where the dreams are half.

Each clang and clatter holds a cheer,
As jugglers toss the shining sphere.
Potatoes break into a song,
In echoes where all things belong.

So grab a friend and hold on tight,
To the absurd, both day and night.
For laughter echoes in the strange,
And makes the mundane feel like change.

Whispers of the Outlandish

In a land where socks can fly with glee,
And umbrellas dance beneath the trees,
Balloons converse with seashells grand,
While lollipop sticks form a band.

A turtle bakes a pie for fun,
As cacti race beneath the sun.
The birds recite a wacky rhyme,
While squirrels play chess in their prime.

The stars giggle in the velvet dark,
Chat about the mysteries of a park.
Chasing dreams on pogo sticks,
In laughter's arms, life gently clicks.

So dare to wander wildly strange,
Embrace the chaos, let life change.
For whispers of the odd and bright,
Will guide us through this curious night.

Strangers in a Strange Land

In a world where sheep wear hats,
And yellow dogs play chess,
I tripped on my own shoelace,
And laughed at my own mess.

The trees were dancing, oh so bold,
While squirrels debated fate,
I asked a cat where dreams are sold,
He said, "Just wait, just wait!"

A penguin slipped upon a slide,
And caused a silly fuss,
While owls played cards, I tried to hide,
From all the laughs around us.

In this realm of quirky sights,
Where nothing's quite the norm,
I found some friends on starry nights,
In laughter, we transform.

Daydreams of the Delightful

I saw a rabbit brewing tea,
In china cups of roses,
He told me tales of jubilee,
And clumsy little posies.

A butterfly in a tuxedo danced,
With flowers as his date,
They stumbled 'round, a love enchanced,
Oh, isn't life just great?

With every sip, the world got bright,
A spoon became a kite,
We soared through clouds of marshmallow white,
In giggles, pure delight.

So join the feast, we'll laugh and cheer,
While jellybeans do sway,
For in this dream, there's naught to fear,
Just blissful games we play.

The Unruly Narrative

Once upon a beetle's shell,
A tale was spun, quite odd,
He wore a cape, and rang a bell,
And sang to every God.

The clocks all melted in the sun,
While cats recited prose,
A circus formed, and just for fun,
The elephants wore clothes.

A fish then took the stage to waltz,
In size fifteen ballet shoes,
He twirled and slipped, oh what a fault!
And offered me his blues.

So gather 'round, embrace the scene,
Where chaos reigns, quite bold,
For in this mad world, we're all unseen,
Just stories left untold.

Fables of the Fantastic

In a garden made of glee,
Grew flowers that sang and danced,
With giggles soft, they pulled me free,
And into whimsy pranced.

A pixie stole my candy cane,
While unicorns wore shades,
They played a game called 'Who's Insane,'
And laughed at all charades.

Each berry burst was filled with cheer,
As cupcakes floated by,
I hopped with joy, and gave a cheer,
For cakes that touched the sky.

So join this fest of silly charms,
Where laughter knows no end,
In stories spun and joyous farms,
You'll find your truest friend.

Absurd Devices of Destiny

In a world of socks that disappear,
Cartwheeling cats might bring us cheer.
Riding bicycles made of cheese,
Laughing at fate with relative ease.

Juggling ducks in the pouring rain,
Trying to dance, but feels like a strain.
Bananas speak in riddles profound,
Lost in a circus spun round and round.

Discovering paths paved in marshmallow,
With dreams that stretch like a rainbow's flow.
Finding a key to a door that won't budge,
All while we smile, we happily trudge.

Tales from the Twilight Zone

In a land where clocks run in reverse,
Each tick and tock a hilarious curse.
Ghosts that bake cookies filled with fear,
Waltzing through echoes, we cheer and jeer.

Dancing shoes that come alive,
Spinning around, we laugh and thrive.
Fish that fly like birds in the air,
Telling us secrets, rich and rare.

Uninvited aliens take our plates,
Making a salad of mismatched traits.
Cups of tea that sing out loud,
In this twilight zone, we're all quite proud.

The Paradoxical Path

Walking on paths of slippery soap,
Finding our balance, testing our hope.
With penguins guiding through tangled vines,
Humor we gain is simply divine.

Maps drawn by toddlers in crayon hues,
Leading us to places we can't refuse.
Hitchhiking with a spoon on a spree,
Each twist and turn brings more glee.

Chasing shadows that giggle and tease,
Echoing laughter flows on the breeze.
Dancing on rooftops, high above,
Finding pure joy in the can't-have-loves.

Joyful Jumbles

In baskets of laughter, we tumble and spin,
Living in moments where chaos begins.
Socks on our hands, they wave and shout,
As the world flips upside down, there's no doubt.

Cheers from a cactus that tells silly jokes,
Mice in top hats playing the folks.
Giraffes on rollercoasters, oh what a sight,
In this merry mishmash, we dance through the night.

Sideways rainbows paint the sky,
Doughnuts on bicycles whizz by.
With each joyful jumble and twist of fate,
We find life's fun is never too late.

Chaotic Footprints

In a world where socks go stray,
I trip on thoughts, led astray.
With mismatched shoes, I run and glide,
Chasing giggles, what a ride!

Spilled coffee on my shirt so bright,
It's art, I claim, not a plight.
Each step a dance, a wobbly beat,
Life's circus can't be beat!

Frogs in hats and cats that sing,
Who knew such joy these quirks could bring?
With laughter wrapping 'round my feet,
I wade through chaos, oh so sweet!

So here's to footprints all askew,
To silly paths, and skies so blue.
In funny moments, we stand tall,
Embracing oddness, laughter's call!

Laughter in the Shadows

In corners dark, where whispers dwell,
Laughter creeps; it casts a spell.
Jokes do pirouettes, masks in hand,
Tickling soft spots, oh so grand!

A squirrel on a bike rides by,
With acorn wheels, it zips, oh my!
In shadows where the oddballs meet,
Laughter lives, a tasty treat!

With giant shoes and funny hats,
Dancing with unpredictable cats.
While life may twist, and time may bend,
In shadows, joy finds its blend.

So let them giggle, let them squeak,
In whispered spaces, joy we seek.
For laughter hides where worries fade,
In absurdity, our joy is laid!

The Oddities of Existence

A banana peel underfoot,
A sudden slip, but what a hoot!
Life's cook never checks the time,
A recipe of chaos, so sublime!

Toasters toast without a care,
While socks conspire away from pairs.
Juggling dreams with jelly beans,
Life's a circus in between!

With pickle hats on turtles' heads,
They boggle thoughts and turn our beds.
Each moment wrapped in zany cheer,
As logic flees, we persevere!

So grab a quirk and wear it proud,
Join in the laughter, sing it loud.
In life's grand farce, let's all partake,
For every giggle, we make no mistake!

Serendipity's Embrace

Stumbling through a field of glee,
I find a spoon beneath a tree.
With universe's gentle shove,
I trip right into pure, sweet love!

A cat in glasses reads a chart,
From clouds to stars, it steals my heart.
While ants debate the meaning of,
Each crumb and crumb, a gentle shove!

Life's a puzzle, pieces stray,
Yet in the chaos, it's okay.
For serendipity's warm embrace,
Brings silly smiles to every place!

So let's toast to the moments odd,
Where laughter's found and lightly trod.
In every twist, life's brightest chance,
Is dancing madly in this dance!

Laughter Echoes in Chaos

In a world where ducks wear hats,
And cats conduct the trains,
We chase our dreams in silly flats,
While laughter drowns our pains.

Jellybeans dance on spaghetti strands,
While time forgets to flow,
The sun flips pancakes, with golden hands,
And clouds put on a show.

Mirrors reflect a playful twirl,
As shoes perform a jig,
We navigate through this wacky swirl,
To humor's witty gig.

So let's embrace the kooky scenes,
With giggles loud and bright,
In chaos, life's absurd routines,
Bring joy and sheer delight.

The Circus of Every Day

Balloons float high in office air,
With clowns that juggle files,
We tiptoe 'round on lion's hair,
And laugh through all the miles.

A tightrope walker on his phone,
Tripping over silly chats,
While elephants wear coats of bone,
And balance books like acrobats.

The ringmaster shouts on a coffee break,
As popcorn flies like cheer,
We twist and twirl for sanity's sake,
In this circus, love appears.

When laughter's the ticket to each new act,
We find the joy in the fray,
In this grand show that we call fact,
Every day's a cabaret.

When Ordinary Meets the Outlandish

A toaster sings to wake the bread,
While socks conspire to hide,
We dance with dust, and dreams instead,
Let weirdness be our guide.

The dog wears glasses, sips his tea,
While ants march off to war,
Talking plants sing songs of glee,
Life never was a bore.

When toast does cartwheels on the plate,
And chairs decide to roll,
We ride the waves of fate so great,
And laughter fills the soul.

So here's to odd and quirky times,
Where chaos finds its flair,
In life's sweet mess, we craft our rhymes,
With joy in every snare.

Grooves in the Fabric of Time

Clock hands dance a jig so spry,
As history DJ's spins,
A rhythm woven, oh so sly,
In laughter, joy begins.

We skate on seconds, twirl with glee,
Through puddles of delight,
As whims tickle, set us free,
In this carousel of light.

A slice of cake, a wink from fate,
With hiccups in the rhyme,
We blend the odd with everyday rate,
Making magic in our prime.

So let the music fill our veins,
And time's absurdity shine,
In grooves of laughter, love remains,
A tapestry divine.

Scribbles on the Map

In a land where logic bends,
I found roads with funny ends.
A triangle leads to a square,
With jellybeans floating in the air.

My compass spins, it plays a tune,
Pointing to a dancing moon.
With every turn, I bump my head,
On signs that say 'Beware of Bread!'

Cows wear glasses, guiding me right,
While fish on bikes zoom past in flight.
A map scribbled by a child's hand,
Leads to treasures made of sand.

And when I stumble on a hill,
I laugh at life's absurd goodwill.
Tomorrow brings a brand new twist,
With shenanigans I can't resist.

The Riddles of Reality

Mirrors crack and laugh with glee,
As gravity flirts with a bumblebee.
Upside down, the sun wears a hat,
While cats engage in chats with a mat.

Time ticks backward for a lark,
With clocks that dance and sing in the park.
Umbrellas bloom beneath the sky,
While cupcakes float and giggle by.

A shoe takes flight; it's quite a sight,
While shadows tango in the night.
Cherry trees with polka dots,
Sprout giggles from their crooked pots.

So chase the riddles, take the dare,
Embrace the madness, hang with care.
In the world where laugh lines grow,
Reality's just a funny show.

Chasing Cuckoo Clouds

I ride on a cloud stitched with dreams,
Where marshmallows float in syrupy streams.
Chasing shadows that tease and play,
With cotton candy skies, I sway.

A parrot recites the news of the day,
While frogs on stilts leap into the fray.
I trip on giggles, slip on a grin,
As ducks in bow ties begin to spin.

The sun wears shades, feeling pretty bold,
While rainbows burst into laughter untold.
I juggle stars, one, two, three,
Falling onto cupcakes, oh, what glee!

So let's frolic where the cuckoos sing,
Dance in circles, let joy take wing.
For life's a stage, and I'm the clown,
In this delightful, topsy-turvy town.

Colors of the Confounding

I paint my thoughts in colors bright,
With purple cats who twirl at night.
A lemon tree that sings a tune,
Beneath a sky of whacky moon.

Magenta fish in a taffy sea,
Invite the tumbleweeds for tea.
While socks do the cha-cha on my floor,
I giggle at what the world has in store.

Upside down, a rainbow's sprout,
Sips lemonade without a doubt.
While clouds throw jellybeans around,
In this art of life, pure joy is found.

So splash your heart with every hue,
Dance through the madness, let it ensue.
For in this chaos, we find our song,
With colors bright, where we all belong.

The Adventure of Misfit Moments

In a world where socks go astray,
Dancing with mismatched shoes today.
Laughter echoes in the street,
As we trip on our own two feet.

A penguin in a summer hat,
Sipping tea while chasing a rat.
Hiccups bring a jolly refrain,
As we stumble through jokes and pain.

The cat plays poker with a crow,
While the sun sets in a neon glow.
Chasing rainbows with no end,
Who knew chaos could be a friend?

With jellybeans stuck in my hair,
I wander through the candy glare.
Every misfit moment, a delight,
In this wacky, wild, silly night.

Lopsided Reflections

Mirrors show the world askew,
Where the clouds are bright and blue.
Wobbling men in funny hats,
Join the dance with cheeky cats.

Puddles laugh as I skip by,
Splashing colors to the sky.
A dragon flies on a skateboard,
While squirrels plot a prank award.

On rooftops, goats are having tea,
Debates of how to prance with glee.
An octopus juggles with flair,
In a circus where no one cares.

The clock melts down the wall again,
Time is wild, like a runaway train.
Life twists and turns with each new bend,
Embrace the madness, it's time to mend.

Tea Parties with Time

At a table made of cheese,
We sip our tea and share some breeze.
With saucers clinking, laughter roars,
As cupcakes dance and knock on doors.

The clock strikes thirteen, what a sight,
With rabbits wearing coats so bright.
Sugar spills like falling stars,
The moon joins in with a few guitars.

We toast to moments lost in space,
While teapots teeter, just in case.
A biscuit giggles, crumbs unfold,
As secrets of our hearts are told.

In this strange, delicious blend,
Where time is both our foe and friend.
Every sip uncovers a grin,
In tea parties where chaos begins.

Catastrophes in Candy Land

In realms of sugar, storms do brew,
Chocolate rivers, bright skies of blue.
Gummy bears don safety hats,
Fighting jellybean acrobats.

A lollipop tree leans to the side,
While the caramel sun begins to glide.
Candy corn falls, like autumn leaves,
In a land where everyone believes.

Spinning tops that fly too high,
Licorice snakes that slyly tie.
Marshmallow clouds start to rain,
As laughter echoes through the grain.

Yet in this land of sweet delight,
Each catastrophe feels just right.
With every mishap, joy we find,
In the wacky world that's free and kind.

The Improv of Existence

In a world that spins round, we dance and we sway,
With socks on our hands, we're leading the way.
Laughter erupts as we trip on the floor,
Who knew mundane life could bring such uproar?

We juggle our fears like flaming balloons,
Balancing dreams under shifting monsoons.
Clowns in the circus, we tumble and play,
Turning mishaps to joy in our silly ballet.

Each twist of fate a slapstick delight,
Chasing our problems into the night.
With puppet strings pulling at hearts all around,
We find a soft landing on folly's grand mound.

So grab your hat and your witty quips,
Join in the laughter, let nonsense eclipse!
For what is a show if not funny and bright?
Let's improvise joy, till we run out of light.

Larks in the Liminal

We sail on a ship that's built from a dream,
With oars made of tacos, we sift through the cream.
The waves laugh along, as we dodge the confetti,
Each splash a reminder, this life ain't too petty.

With jellybean maps, we navigate fate,
Finding treasure in puddles, we call it our fate.
The toast starts to dance while we sip on the breeze,
As laughter erupts from the oddest of glees.

We taxied on clouds, made coffee from stars,
Played chess with the moon, while counting our scars.
Each little quirk in this curious ride,
Is a twist in the tale where we laugh and abide.

So here's to the larks, in this limbo we roam,
With pockets of whimsy, we build our own home.
For what's life without giggles or a little surprise?
Let's wade through the absurd with wide-open eyes.

Melodies of the Madcap

In the symphony of chaos, we hum out of tune,
With recorders that squawk like a ragged raccoon.
The world's a grand stage, where the clowns take the lead,
Conducting with relish the wildness we need.

Each note a reminder of laughter's sweet call,
As we stumble and wiggle, refusing to fall.
The baton made of spaghetti we wave to the sky,
With melodies woven from mischief, oh my!

So come join the concert, bring your trumpet of cheese,
In this orchestra's madness, we do just as we please.
With cymbals of giggles, and a chorus of fun,
Life dances around us, till the day is all done.

With a wink and a nod, we embrace the strange song,
In notes filled with laughter, we find where we belong.
Let's march to the rhythm of whims' sweet parade,
In the melodies of madcap, let's never be afraid.

The Peculiar Pilgrim

Here walks a pilgrim, with shoes on the wrong,
Counting each misstep, oblivious to song.
With a map made of napkins, and snacks for the road,
He finds that the bumps are just life's little code.

Through valleys of chaos, he strolls with delight,
With jelly on toast and a hat that's too tight.
He skips past the worries, the frowns and the haste,
Finding joy in the hiccups, it's never a waste.

In a world filled with quirks, he taps to the beat,
Inventing new dances while searching for feet.
With sprinkles of laughter and shoes covered in goo,
He tiptoes through life, in his own joyful zoo.

So here's to the pilgrim, embracing each twist,
With stories that linger, too fun to resist.
For every odd turn leads to a grin,
Let's celebrate life's madness—come join in the spin!

Tumbling Through Time

We skip on clouds that smell like cheese,
Chasing shadows on the breeze.
Tick-tock goes the silly clock,
Stopping for tea with a dancing rock.

Sideways glances at upside-down,
A jester's hat, a king's old crown.
Through puddles of giggles, we slip and slide,
With rubber ducks as our guide.

The planets spin in mismatched shoes,
While squirrels serenade with ridiculous tunes.
In every blink, a twist of fate,
We laugh and play, it's never too late.

With every whirl, the world's anew,
As hiccuping hosts serve chocolate stew.
Life's a carnival, silly and fun,
Under the brightly-painted sun.

The Irreverent Road

There's a road paved with candy and peanut butter,
Where llamas jive and voices flutter.
A compass spins in a dizzy whirl,
Pointing to cupcakes that giggle and twirl.

We skip with socks of mismatched hues,
Telling tall tales of daring moose.
On this trail of the outlandish and bright,
Every wrong turn feels perfectly right.

With rainbows painted by careless hands,
Puppets dance to the tune of bands.
The sun wears shades, looking quite suave,
While shadows do the cha-cha with suave.

In the whirl of oddities, we choose to roam,
Distanced from norms, we call this home.
The world's a stage with nudges and quirks,
With laughter weaving through all of its works.

Nonsense and Nuance

In a land where the clocks climb trees,
I sip my tea as fish learn to breeze.
A cat in a tie gives lessons in grace,
While squirrels debate the best food pace.

Nonsense reigns, and logic's a play,
With every thought turning oddball today.
A sprinkle of whimsy, a dash of flair,
Life's a circus, come join with a dare!

The moon fancies hats made of cheese,
Starfish read tales in whips of the seas.
As ducks on stilts waddle about,
The world spins on; who needs a route?

With giggles and wiggles, we shift through the haze,
In the chaos of clarity, we dance and we blaze.
Life's a puzzle where pieces may miss,
Yet every twist is a reason for bliss.

The Cacophony of Choices

Amidst the noise of clattering dreams,
We wade through puddles of silly schemes.
Every nudge brings a brand new laugh,
On paths where logic chose to take a bath.

With jellybeans stuck in every gear,
The choices echo, loud but clear.
Should I pick blue or radical green?
In the symphony of chaos, all things glean.

A parrotlicious puppet sings off-key,
While dancing to rhythms of pure jubilee.
In this cacophony, there's joy to be found,
Like spinning in circles on playgrounds around!

So let the ruckus be a sweet serenade,
With laughter as our trusty brigade.
In the cacophony, we dance and we play,
Who needs a map for this wild escapade?

The Kaleidoscope of Strange

In a world where socks have moods,
And pigeons plot at noon,
I trip on thoughts like balloons,
While my cat plays a tune.

Bananas jog in tired shoes,
Chasing lemons with a grin,
The clock sings loudly in blues,
As I dance with my gin.

Frogs in hats sip elder tea,
Debating which hat is best,
While I wonder, oh can it be,
This madness feels like a jest?

So here's to the quirky and bold,
With each twist and every bend,
Life's a story to unfold,
Where absurdities never end.

Oddities on the Path Less Travelled

There's a snail teaching yoga on a hill,
While toadstools check their styles,
I've seen hats engage in a battle,
As squirrels run election miles.

A giraffe reads poetry on a fence,
While frogs compose a play,
Each wiggle and leap feels intense,
As we laugh the day away.

Umbrella birds fly upside down,
While crickets hold a rave,
The whispers of the merry town,
Fill paths that misbehave.

So I stroll with a bottle of dreams,
Where nonsense leads the chase,
In this curious land of seams,
Absurdity's warm embrace.

Juggling Dreams in a Mad World

With juggling beans and singing pies,
I'm in a circus of the weird,
As llamas in tutus twirl and rise,
While I face my biggest fear!

The clouds wear coats of polka dots,
As rainbows flip on cue,
The squirrels share their secret plots,
To bake a cake anew.

Gumdrops dance upon the grass,
While ice-cream cones conspire,
Each bizarre moment comes to pass,
A feast of joy that won't tire.

I laugh in this carnival of glee,
With dreams tossed in the air,
Life's a juggling act for me,
With absurdity everywhere!

The Laughing Compass

A compass spins in silly glee,
Pointing west to oxen's chat,
With wind-up ducks that sip on tea,
While I chase an absent cat.

The road's erased with jellybeans,
Each step I take feels sweet,
The sun has legs, it hops and preens,
As nonsense greets my feet.

I twists and tumble through this play,
Where giggles light the way,
A dance of whimsy leads my day,
In laughter, I wish to stay.

So I trust my compass made of jest,
As it spins me round with flair,
In follies where absurdities rest,
I'll follow laughter everywhere!

The Whimsy of Wandering Thoughts

A sock once said to a shoe,
"Why must I always be blue?"
The shoe replied with a grin,
"You've got to learn to let in the win!"

A cat wore a hat made of cheese,
Dancing around with whimsical ease.
The mouse was quite taken aback,
Screaming, "Oh no, I'm under attack!"

Fish walked the streets on parade,
In sunglasses, they never would fade.
They flipped and flopped past the park,
To show the world they're a little stark!

So, let's skip with joy on this road,
Where laughter's the lightest of load.
Join the absurd, don't miss the fun,
In this circus act, we're never done!

Eccentricities in Everyday Life

An umbrella decided to fly,
With dreams to kiss the bright sky.
It floated then landed on a frog,
Who croaked, "Now isn't this quite the slog?"

A toaster danced with a loaf of bread,
"You toast my heart!" it bravely said.
The jar of jam chimed in with glee,
"And I'm just here for the harmony!"

The clock struck twelve, then sneezed so loud,
Leaving all the hours quite cowed.
A tick-tock echo through the room,
Announced that chaos would now bloom!

In this realm of odd and strange,
Where routines flex and gently change,
Let's giggle through each quirky bruise,
And find joy in this grand amusement cruise!

Wandering Through Whimsy

A hedgehog wore a top hat, oh dear,
As it strolled down the pavement beer.
Sipping tea with a rubber duck,
Both giggled at the world's strange luck.

A pancake flipped high in the air,
Screamed, "Catch me if you dare!"
The syrup quivered in fear and delight,
Wishing for flavors that felt just right!

The sun decided to wear shades of pink,
While the clouds formed a line for a drink.
Each raindrop wished for a chance to play,
Creating puddles where kids can sway!

So let's twirl like leaves in the breeze,
Chasing absurdities with utmost ease.
In this carnival of laughter, who knows?
Life's a waltz through the highs and the lows!

The Dance of Doubt

A chicken danced with a confused cow,
"What are we doing?" the cow asked, wow!
The chicken clucked, "Just flow with the beat,
Life's just a grand, mischievous treat!"

An artist painted with noodles and gold,
Creating masterpieces, brave and bold.
While spaghetti swirled with a twist in the air,
Forming a portrait of a grizzly bear!

A sigh was heard from a lazy chair,
"Do I lounge or join? It's quite the affair!"
But the table just shrugged, with a wobble, a laugh,
"Just sit back, my friend, enjoy the craft!"

In the whimsical dance of what's true,
Doubt pirouettes, but that's nothing new.
So let's tiptoe lightly and laugh all around,
For in the absurd, joy is always found!

When Reality Takes a Detour

The toaster sings while bread takes flight,
A squirrel in glasses reads by candlelight.
Cats wear hats and dance at dawn,
While chairs discuss the best way to yawn.

Clouds wear pants, the sun dons a tie,
Mice play chess as roaches sigh.
Reality's map is a jigsaw puzzle,
Each piece a giggle, a joyful shuffle.

What's real, what's not, a blurred line we tread,
Pigeons recite poetry, we all shake our heads.
A bicycle rides a bike, too, it's true,
In this world of jest, the surreal feels new.

Chasing the logic that always seems bent,
We laugh at the things that make no real sense.
So hop on a ride that's spinning so tight,
And let's keep on laughing till far after night.

Fragments of the Bizarre

A fish in a bowtie swims through the trees,
Mice bake cupcakes with dance and with ease.
An octopus juggles dreams in the park,
While shadows debate how to leave a remark.

Socks with two left feet strut down the road,
While umbrellas discuss their weathered old code.
Toasters and kettles share secrets so sly,
As shoes in the closet conspire to fly.

An elephant tap-dances on stilts made of cheese,
And squirrels converse while enjoying the breeze.
The humor unfolds in the things out of place,
In this merry-go-round of absurdity's grace.

So pluck a string from the fabric of cheer,
And let the oddities draw ever near.
Each laugh that we share is a gift from the heart,
In this grand orchestra, we all play a part.

The Carnival of Quirks

Step right up, see the juggling giraffe,
It's selling popcorn while taking a bath.
Clowns ride bicycles made out of fruit,
As singers croon tunes from a giant boot.

The ringmaster's hat is a huge strawberry,
While monkeys steal peanuts, a merry old fairy.
A dunk tank for dreams in a bucket of tears,
As laughter and joy drown out all our fears.

The merry-go-round spins with a song of the wise,
While dragons pretend they can juggle the skies.
Sea turtles whisper, sharing tales of delight,
As the moon paints the tent with a silvery light.

So join in the dance of this quirky parade,
Where fun meets the logic that often just fades.
For laughter is magic, a colorful spark,
That brightens our path in the realm of the dark.

Sundrops in a Storm

Raindrops tap-dance on rooftops so gray,
While umbrellas join in, swirling away.
A snail sells sunshine to worms in the dirt,
As puddles play chess in the grass with a flirt.

Clouds wear polka dots and giggle on high,
Each lightning bolt winks, a flash in the sky.
Kites fly backwards in an aerial race,
Tangled in laughter, they wobble with grace.

In the midst of the storm, a rainbow appears,
With each color laughing, dispersing our fears.
The wind tells a joke that we can't quite recall,
While trees shake their leaves in a whimsical thrall.

So grab your galoshes, skip puddles with glee,
For even the storms hold a sweet, funny spree.
In life's wildest moments, joy tries to conform,
And we find sundrops sparkling even in storm.

Embracing the Uncertain

Woke up to find my socks mismatched,
The coffee pot's broken, but who's attached?
Life's a circus, clowns in a line,
Juggling woes, sipping on lemon-lime.

The car won't start, it vrooms like a cat,
Sailed on a bike with a quirky hat.
Riding the waves of this whimsical tide,
Laughing at things that we can't decide.

Serenade of the Silly

Dancing with shadows, they step on my toes,
Chasing my dreams while I trip on my woes.
A pigeon sings opera while I steal a glance,
The sun wears a bow tie, inviting a dance.

Bananas on scooters, the fruit's got the moves,
While I'm trying to figure out my own grooves.
Laughter's the ticket to this wild parade,
Join in the folly, let worries degrade.

Curiosities Along the Path

Found a blue feather, it whispered my name,
A cat offered wisdom, but forgot the game.
Frogs wearing glasses discuss worldly views,
While I'm caught in the moment, fumbling my shoes.

Clouds are debating if they're cake or fluff,
As I navigate chaos, still laughing enough.
Life's quirks in a basket, I'll carry them through,
With every odd sighting, there's joy to renew.

The Eccentric Mosaic

Colors are scattered, no picture in sight,
An artist with jokes makes the canvas bright.
Crayons are talking, each color a muse,
While reality giggles, we've nothing to lose.

Worms in top hats hold a tea party near,
As I sip on giggles and conquer my fear.
This patchwork of nonsense, my heart is its thread,
In a world so absurd, I smile instead.

Balloons and Broken Wishes

Balloons float high, oh so bright,
Chasing dreams in mid-flight.
But a gust can pop, what a sight,
Leaving wishes in the night.

Silly hats worn askew,
Dance with joy, we twirl and skew.
Funny faces, what a crew,
In this circus, it's all true.

Pie on faces, laughter loud,
We become the silliest crowd.
Life's a joke, we laugh so proud,
Crowned in joy, beneath the cloud.

So let's embrace the chaos here,
With giggles, jokes, and lots of cheer.
For in the mess, we persevere,
And turn the strange into sincere.

The Ridiculous Rhapsody

Life's a tune, all out of key,
With rhythm shown, it's plain to see.
Tangled strings can set us free,
As we waltz beneath the tree.

Hats that wobble, shoes that squeak,
Silly antics, no need to peak.
In this dance, the lost can seek,
Joyful giggles as we sneak.

Twirling round on one long sock,
Time ticks slowly with each block.
Laughter echoes, what a shock,
Each mishap becomes a rock.

Let's compose a raucous cheer,
Embrace the strange with no more fear.
In nonsense, clarity seems near,
Life's a song that we hold dear.

Ephemeral Peculiarities

Clouds of cotton candy swirl,
Tickling hearts in a crazy whirl.
Wit and whimsy gently unfurl,
In a world where dreams can twirl.

Owls in hats say, "What a sight!"
Chasing shadows in the night.
With each laugh, we feel so light,
Absurdity is pure delight.

A jester's leap, a tumble down,
Laughter brightens every frown.
In this circus, we've been crowned,
As joyful clowns, we spin around.

Memories made in fleeting time,
In the quirky, we find our rhyme.
Oh, the beauty of the climb,
In the odd, life's perfect mime.

Unruly Threads of Experience

Stitches of joy, woven with care,
Each loop a laugh, floating in air.
Barefoot we go, without a scare,
In the tapestry of life, we share.

Strings that tangle, colors clash,
Nosey gnomes watch as we dash.
Tripping on dreams, we hit a splash,
With every twist, there's no need to brash.

Life's a quilt, sewn with mischief,
Each patch a tale, some bring grief.
Yet we smile, finding relief,
In the absurd, our common belief.

So let's embrace each weird turn,
For in the strange, there's much to learn.
With humor's spark, we brightly burn,
In life's grand show, we take our turn.